Contents

Note: For the purposes of this book, the pupil is referred to as 'he' and the teacher as 'she'.

Chapter One

Why This Tour?

There is a wealth of books about Special Educational Needs (SEN) on the market today. Many of them contain excellent detailed information about specific difficulties. You can find books written by medics, psychologists and educationalists on subjects such as autism spectrum disorders, dyslexia, dyspraxia, learning difficulties, physical and sensory disabilities, and social, emotional and behavioural difficulties. They make highly recommended reading for the professional who wishes to gain greater knowledge in specialised areas.

This book, however, is written for a wider audience.

For the past decade or more, but particularly since the SEN and Disability Act of 2001, and the Standards in Scotland's Schools etc. Act (2000), with its emphasis on inclusion, equal entitlement and a presumption of mainstreaming, the expectation is that the majority of pupils with any kind of Special Educational Need will now have the right to be educated in their local mainstream school. The training implications of this for teachers and their assistants are, of course, huge. Historically, the staff in special schools were the only ones who really needed knowledge and expertise in SEN. Pupils who were in mainstream but not coping would be quickly transferred out. However, the move towards inclusion now means that all mainstream teachers and teaching assistants need to have at least a basic knowledge and understanding about the wide range of difficulties listed in the first paragraph, all of which they may encounter in their classes at some point during their career. They also need to develop the expertise to help them enable their pupils to access learning and meet their educational needs.

The purpose of this book is to help mainstream staff achieve this.

It will take you on a journey into the fascinating world of SEN and provide you with core information about pupils' difficulties, give you useful strategies, show you around the educational structures, help you understand essential jargon and give you some top tips for survival! If you read nothing else on the subject (and we sincerely hope that this book will whet your appetite to do so), then at least you will have a fundamental overview of SEN which we hope will help you succeed in your career.

Therefore, if you are reading this book you are likely to be either a newly qualified teacher or a teaching assistant keen to learn about SEN. You might also be someone who has been in education for some time but has had little need, up until now, to know much about SEN. This book has been born out of a recognition by the authors (both of whom are current practitioners), of the need for an easily readable, user-friendly, practical guide to help staff in schools.

A 'whistle-stop tour' implies covering a great distance but stopping only briefly at different places. This 'Whistle-Stop Tour of SEN' will do exactly that, visiting many places but stopping only fleetingly at each one.

So let's begin our journey here ...

Shakespeare once wrote, '*A rose by any other name would smell as sweet*'.

Nowhere is this more true than in the world of SEN. Looking back in time, the vocabulary used to describe people with SEN has included many derogatory terms. Thankfully, these days are past, and our understanding and knowledge of disabilities has increased immensely over the past hundred years. At the same time societal attitudes have become much more enlightened, and we are working towards a greater acceptance of other people's differences, whatever they may be.

Over the past few decades, we have gone through a range of educational terminology to describe pupils with SEN. They have been referred to as mentally handicapped, mentally subnormal, educationally subnormal, remedial pupils, pupils with learning disabilities, pupils with learning difficulties and now we currently use the all encompassing term of pupils who have Special Educational Needs. This includes all those who have difficulties accessing the curriculum for whatever reason, whether that difficulty is physical, sensory, communication, language, learning, social or emotional.

The Special Educational Needs Code of Practice (2001) for England and Wales, which will be more fully discussed later, states that:

'Children have special educational needs if they have a *learning difficulty* which calls for *special educational provision* to be made for them.'

The Code goes on to define what is meant as a learning difficulty by stating,

'Children have a *learning difficulty* if they:

    a) have a significantly greater difficulty in learning than the majority of children of the same age; or

    b) have a disability which prevents or hinders them from making use of educational facilities of a kind generally provided for children of the same age in schools within the area of the local education authority.

The Code continues by defining the term special educational provision as:

    a) for children of two or over, educational provision which is additional to, or otherwise different from, the educational provision made generally for children of their age in schools maintained by the LEA, other than special schools, in the area.

In Scotland, similar statements were contained in the Education (Scotland) Act (1980) and further defined in the 1994 Report 'Effective Provision for Special Educational Needs' (EPSEN). It stated that:

    a) most special educational needs arise from curricular difficulties caused by a mismatch between the delivery of the curriculum and pupils' learning needs

    b) other special educational needs may arise from disabilities creating difficulties in, and barriers to, learning

    c) social and emotional factors may also affect a pupil's capacity to learn.

It is worth taking note of these definitions at this early point in the book so that these key terms are very clear.

Chapter Two

Inclusion

But now our first stopping point is 'Inclusion' and a brief glance into recent history will help us better understand the process.

The drive to promote a more inclusive education system in the UK began with the publication of the Warnock Report in 1978. A committee, chaired by Mary Warnock, was set up with the task of revising the system of education which was in place at that time for children with SEN. Up until the seventies, these children were often deemed to be 'uneducable' in any academic sense, and were placed in establishments known as Junior or Senior Training Centres. These were staffed by either qualified or unqualified Instructors, but who were not necessarily qualified teachers. The quality of training or education that these children received was extremely variable. Expectation of achievement was very low, and the focus of the training in these centres was usually on tasks of a practical nature, for example, woodwork or needlework, rather than any academic skills. One of the outcomes of the Warnock Report was to ensure that all children were entitled to a broad and balanced education which included academic and practical subjects and which mirrored a mainstream curriculum. The Training Centres with their old staffing structures and systems were phased out and became known as 'Special Schools' which were staffed by qualified teachers.

Initially, these schools often catered for a quite specific group of children who shared the same needs. For example, there were schools for pupils with a physical disability, a visual or hearing impairment, for children with autism, and those with behavioural difficulties. Children had learning difficulties, which were classified as being either moderate or severe, and attended a school which catered specifically for their level of need. Those children with the most profound disabilities were placed in special care units within the special school. It was usual for most pupils to remain in their special provision throughout their school life and opportunities for social or academic inclusion were not generally available.

In addition to the Warnock Report in 1978, a report on pupils with learning difficulties was published in Scotland by H. M. Inspectors. The Progress Report, as it became known, was significant in identifying the curriculum and the way it was planned and implemented as the major cause of learning difficulties. It argued that difficulties arising in ordinary classrooms were best addressed there, rather than removing the pupil from the class. It recommended a restructuring of the remedial service in mainstream schools into a Learning Support Service. Learning Support teachers received specialist training and were expected to work with class or subject teachers, pupils and other professionals to support the learning for all pupils. The Report defined four clear roles for Learning Support teachers:

a) Consultancy

b) Co-operative teaching

c) Direct tuition

d) Specialist services.

As the Learning Support Service developed during the 1980s a fifth role – that of Staff Development - was also added. Teachers were encouraged to view the *curriculum* as problematic and requiring adaptation through differentiation, rather than viewing the child as a problem to be removed elsewhere.

Thus Warnock and the Progress Report had started a process of change which would only gather momentum.

The rigid selection procedure when deciding a special school placement for pupils was beginning to relax. This was partly due to the sheer practicalities and expense of transporting pupils by taxi or mini bus long distances round the county to get to their specialist schools. Special schools, therefore, became more generic, becoming able to admit pupils with a range of difficulties. They discovered that there were also some benefits to integrating pupils who had different difficulties.

In 1994, countries from around the world gathered in Salamanca, in Spain, to discuss the way forward on issues of disability and inclusion in society in response to the 1989 United Nations Convention on the Rights of the Child, and of course this had huge implications for our educational systems. There was a hope and an expectation that by educating all children together, no matter what their differences, we could learn to live together, embracing each other without prejudice.

Strong influences such as these, together with bold initiatives in some Local Education Authorities (LEAs) and increased parental choice resulted in more pupils with SEN being educated in mainstream schools. But still, across the UK, there was inconsistency in the quality of provision for some of these pupils. The quality of provision a pupil received in a local school might be more dependent on his postcode than on anything else.

Developments in England and Wales

In 1994 the Government in England and Wales published the 'The Special Educational Needs Code of Practice', which outlined a school's statutory obligations to pupils and parents and gave practical advice on how best to support their pupils with SEN. Three years later, in 1997, the Green Paper, 'Excellence for all Children – Meeting Special Educational Needs' set out government plans to ensure that all children with SEN had the best possible chance of reaching their full potential.

The Code of Practice was then revised in 2001, a year which also saw the introduction of the SEN and Disability Act. This law ensured inclusion for all.

Three years later, in 2004, the Government published a strategy, 'Removing Barriers to Achievement', which would fine tune some of the issues in the 2001 Act which still needed addressing, such as the uneven provision of resources, expertise, training and support available to pupils with SEN in mainstream schools across the country.

Developments in Scotland

In 1994 the Scottish Office Education Department published a report by H.M. Inspectorate 'Effective Provision for Special Educational Needs' (EPSEN). This consolidated and updated the ideas contained in both the Warnock and Progress Reports of 1978. It identified ten key features of effective practice for pupils with SEN, and emphasised that the five roles of Support for Learning applied to all SEN specialist staff. In 1998 it was supplemented by the Scottish Office publication 'A Manual of Good Practice'.

In 1999 the advent of a Scottish Parliament with devolved powers for education led to a commitment to developing inclusion. In 2000 the five National Priorities in Education were published including one on Inclusion and Equality while The Standards in Scotland's Schools etc. Act (2000) contained a specific emphasis on inclusion, equal entitlement and a presumption of mainstreaming. This legislation was required to be implemented by education authorities by August 2003.

In 2002 the Education (Disability Strategies and Pupils' Educational Records) Act was passed. This requires local authorities and other education providers to prepare and implement strategies to ensure that disabled pupils have improved access to the curriculum, physical access and access to information.

In 2004 the Education (Additional Support for Learning) (Scotland) Act was passed and is due to come into effect in autumn 2005. At that point, references in law to 'special educational needs' will cease in Scotland.

The Act introduces a new framework built around the concept of *additional support needs* and will apply to any child or young person who requires extra support for whatever reason. It firmly shifts the emphasis from '*the individual child as a problem*' to one of entitlement and provides a framework of support and range of strategies to address that entitlement for learners and their families.

A Code of Practice, to be published in summer 2005, will provide guidance for local authorities and other agencies to promote more effective joint planning and partnerships.

So let's take a moment to stop and see where that leaves us now.

Firstly, it is important to remember that the view still varies from authority to authority. However, generally, most authorities are aiming to reduce the number of pupils who are educated in Special Schools. The expectation is that, wherever possible and practical, pupils with SEN will attend their local mainstream school. Most LEAs have established systems of specialist support to help these schools. Teams of highly qualified and experienced teachers will visit schools where staff are needing advice on a particular disability or help with a particular pupil. Generally, a pupil will be placed in a special school only where their needs are so great that it would be detrimental to their own progress or the progress of their peers for them to remain in a mainstream class.

Hopefully then, having examined the recent history of Special Education we can more fully understand the context of the situation we find ourselves in today. Let's now move forward and bring our focus into the classroom itself.

Chapter Three

Challenging
Our Assumptions!

First of all, let's challenge our assumptions.

In order to have a smooth and comfortable journey we need to clear any obstacles that may lie in our path. As far as working with pupils with SEN is concerned, we must look at our assumptions and be prepared to challenge them. Any assumptions which are not helpful must be removed.

So what might they be? Let's look at some which are frequently held but which the enlightened teacher or teaching assistant will want to examine carefully. They are listed below but are not in any deliberate order and they are followed by the main reasons why these assumptions do not necessarily hold good for pupils with SEN, although they may sometimes be appropriately applied to the average mainstream pupil.

The assumption that your pupils will be at the same developmental starting point.

All pupils will develop and learn at different rates and will reach different stages at different times. The reasons for this are many and varied and can include health, gender, inherent physical, cognitive and language developmental rates, background and environment. These differences will be accentuated in pupils with difficulties of any kind and the greater the degree of difficulty or disability, the more necessary it is for us to cast out all assumptions about starting points.

 The assumption that all pupils will have the same knowledge.

We can never be sure exactly how much any pupil has been previously taught, nor how much they have been able to learn (for whatever reason). Even assessments only show what that pupil is capable of achieving at any one given moment in time. Where a pupil has inherent difficulties of any nature, their ability to access the curriculum and learn efficiently is likely to have been reduced. Pupils with medical conditions will have probably missed out whole chunks of their education. Therefore, teachers must recognise that each pupil's knowledge base is likely to be unique and must consequently be prepared to accommodate that fact.

 The assumption that because pupils have experienced something before, they will automatically remember it.

Memory is crucially important in the learning process. No matter what has been taught or experienced, if the pupil is not able to retain that information then they will have difficulties building up further skills. Many pupils with a learning difficulty of any kind display a poor working, or short-term, memory. Teachers may need to be prepared to build in to a pupil's programme many opportunities for practice or over-learning of previously taught work, in order to try and place it more permanently into his long-term memory.

The assumption that all pupils can understand the language that is being used around them.

It is likely that many pupils with SEN will have a difficulty with some area of language. They may have a problem in processing language which can lead to poor receptive skills (the ability to understand language) or poor expressive skills (the ability to formulate language and communicate it to others). In addition, some pupils may have a problem with their speech or articulation. Pupils who have a social communication difficulty will by definition have problems understanding the social use of language. Therefore it is absolutely essential for the mainstream teacher to try to ascertain the level of language ability of her special needs pupils so she can modify her own language when teaching them and set time aside in their programme for extra help in understanding the content of lessons. The skilful teaching assistant will be able to provide the interface between the class teacher and pupil in the area of language.

 The assumption that pupils will have the gross motor or fine motor skills to carry out certain tasks.

Pupils may not have adequately co-ordinated gross motor skills, i.e. large physical movement abilities such as running, jumping, climbing stairs, etc., and fine motor skills, i.e. smaller physical movement skills usually associated with the upper body, hands and arms. Poor fine motor skills affect handwriting, cutting, drawing, dressing and undressing, etc. Of course it should be quite clear that any pupil with a diagnosed physical disability will not be as efficient at motor tasks as their peers, but it should also be noted that many other more conditions can be accompanied by associated motor difficulties.

The assumption that all pupils enjoy social interaction.

Schools are places where socialising activities and teamwork are encouraged both through the daily curriculum and in extra curricular activities. Some pupils with SEN find these situations difficult and stressful. Pupils on the autism spectrum will almost certainly find the socialising aspect of school life confusing, and at times, stressful. Teachers should be aware of the need for such pupils to have a quiet place where they can withdraw. On the other hand, pupils with emotional and social difficulties can also find correct socialisation hard and therefore don't always enjoy it.

The assumption that all pupils will understand and respect the school's standards of behaviour.

Pupils come from all walks of life and the expectations of home and school might be different. Most schools have certain agreed standards of behaviour which might, in fact, be quite alien to some pupils. While it is part of a school's role to teach pupils to be polite, well mannered and considerate of other people, those pupils who may not have known such an ethos in their own home background will find it much harder to adapt and conform than others for whom these standards are familiar and consistent throughout their lives. Pupils' own experiences of life will contribute to the way they respond and react to others. Teachers might find that some pupils will require direct teaching in social skills and this should be borne in mind when planning pupils' programmes.

The importance of a teacher *not* having preconceived ideas about her pupils cannot be over emphasised.

However, a lack of knowledge of pupils' difficulties can also create the same misunderstandings. The teacher or teaching assistant must make themselves aware of any difficulties already noted in reports and then research information about these. Armed with a little more knowledge they will be able to see the challenge of school life from the perspective of the pupil, which in turn will determine their own response to him.

Chapter Four

Different Perspectives from an Imaginary Class

Let's stop for a moment and see what these two different perspectives, that of the pupil and that of the teacher, might look like …

Imagine this, it's your first day working in a new school. You are full of enthusiasm for your new job and looking forward to the challenge. You may just be with one class, if you are working in a Primary school (an easier scenario), or you could be working with a number of classes of different age groups if you are in a secondary school (a little more difficult).

After your first day has finished, you take time to reflect. This is how it might have seemed to you ...

Amy was fine all the time that the class was discussing the topic and contributed well verbally. She even asked some interesting questions which really impressed you. When you asked the class to go and write down what they had learnt, Amy sat at her desk and did almost nothing. She said she didn't have a pen and when she was given one, she sat and fiddled with it. You couldn't understand why she couldn't get started and write down what she so obviously knew. You felt that by the end of the lesson she had achieved very little and you were disappointed with her effort.

Joe was unable to sit still throughout most of the lesson, especially during the whole class session. He distracted others by fidgeting, making noises, and interrupted you constantly by shouting out a mixture of correct answers and totally irrelevant comments. He also tended to wander around the classroom when he should have been doing his written work. You found this both frustrating and irritating, especially as you could tell that he had grasped the main points of the lesson. Unfortunately, his behaviour was affecting both your teaching and the other pupils' learning.

Sarah refused to work with any other pupils, even though you tried to choose the groups carefully. You asked her several times to join the group, but she stayed sitting where she was. When you attempted to talk to her, she refused to look at you, put her head down and bit her finger. After a while, she wandered over to another group and sat with them. You were at a loss to know what to do, and ended up leaving her where she was.

David tried really hard during the whole lesson and got on quietly with his work. However, when you collected the work in, you were quite surprised because you could hardly read what was written on the page. The handwriting was virtually illegible and there were only a few lines of it. You make a note that you will have to remind him about neatness next time.

Lucy seemed to have difficulty with the lesson right from the start. She couldn't concentrate; was eager to answer, but her answers were often unrelated to the question. She didn't seem to be able to do anything independently, and you had to constantly remind her of what to do next. You ended up writing a lot of the work down for her to copy, so she could get it done. Even then, she had made many errors.

Frankie seemed to have difficulty following your instructions. At the beginning of the lesson you told the whole class what you wanted them to do. Frankie looked at you a bit blankly; you asked him if he knew what he was supposed to be doing and he shook his head. It appeared as if he hadn't understood what you were saying. When you told him again in a different way, he did it. You noticed that when you were talking to the whole class, Frankie gazed out of the window and didn't seem interested.

Jordan, you hope, was just having a bad day. Right from the start you knew he was there. He came into the classroom swearing at another pupil because he thought they'd pushed him. He constantly kicked his chair and wouldn't stop even though you'd asked him to several times. He refused to do any writing at first, going as far as snapping his pencil. At the end of the lesson he ripped up the small amount of work he had done, claiming it was rubbish. You felt that you had been ineffective in dealing with his behaviours and that he seemed to have a lot of problems.

Annabel was wearing a hearing aid. She came up to you before the start of the lesson to give you the radio microphone. She was confident and explained to you how to use it. You were very aware of her throughout the lesson, making sure you were facing her when you spoke, and checking that she was able to hear and understand.

Let's now reflect on what you might be thinking or how you might be feeling after this first day's experience. Apart from feeling rather tired, maybe, you could be feeling challenged by the diversity of the pupils in the class. Several of them responded in unexpected ways and you are wondering why.

But … how might your pupils be reflecting on that very first same day working with *you*? These could be *their* thoughts …

Amy … 'I liked listening to the lesson. I was quite interested in what she was saying, and I know I was quite good at answering the questions, but then she asked us to do some writing. I don't know why but I just can't do the writing. The letters all seem to get jumbled up, I write them the wrong way round and I can't do the spellings. I really hate it when I get it all wrong, even though I try hard, and it makes me feel like crying.'

Joe … 'I knew we were going to have someone new today, but I didn't know what she would be like. She was OK but she talked a lot and kept getting on to me because she said I wasn't listening. It's really difficult to sit still and I wanted to talk to my friends. I like it when I know the answer to a question, but I forget the rules and just want to be the first to tell the teacher. I hate sitting in my chair for a long time and it makes me feel better if I walk around the class a bit, but I get told off a lot for this. I can never wait till break when I can play football with my friends.'

Sarah ... 'She hadn't said we were going to work in groups, so I didn't know. Anyway, I don't like Ben because he has glasses and I'm not working with him. She tried to make me look at her; what for? Just to see her face getting red? I began to get cross, so I started biting my finger; that helps me. I felt better then, so I went to sit next to Joanne because I like Joanne.'

David ... 'I try hard but my writing is always messy. I bet she tells me next time to be neater, but I can't. My fingers hurt after a while and I have to stop. Everybody else can write lots more than me and neater too. I like it when we get to use the computer because then my writing looks like everybody else's.'

Lucy ... 'I like the new lady; she helped me a lot. She even wrote it all down for me to copy. She wanted me to write it by myself, like the others, but I couldn't. It's OK as long as she doesn't ask me to read what I've written, because reading is hard. I didn't really understand the lesson, but I copied nearly as much writing as my friend, and she's clever.'

Frankie ... 'Why do grown-ups always talk so much and use such hard words? At the beginning I try to listen, but I just can't seem to follow what they say. I get so lost that I give up and think my own thoughts. I often get told off for daydreaming and looking out of the window. Today she told us all what to do, but I didn't understand at first. It was better when she came and spoke to me on my own and then I knew what she meant.'

Jordan ... 'I hate school. What's the point? I can't do the work. Nobody likes me. People always seem to get me into trouble and the adults are always picking on me. I don't expect she will be any different; she let me get away with it today. Mr Jones, he's OK, because he's strict but you know he's fair.'

> Annabel … 'I had a good day. The new lady was OK. Although I don't think she had seen a radio microphone before, it was fine.'

The temptation is often to only see things from our own point of view. This is quite natural, but the challenge of this book is to encourage those of us working with pupils to ask ourselves why they might respond and react as they do. Understanding the nature and extent of their difficulties is in fact the key to moving forward with positive solutions.

So let's just take a second look at our pupils, this time armed with a little more understanding and knowledge.

> Amy presents as a pupil who has obvious difficulties with literacy. However, orally she is quite able and in these situations she copes well and is motivated. Problems arise when she is required to write anything down on paper. She has developed good avoidance strategies, e.g. fiddling with her pen rather than writing, because she knows that she cannot succeed at the task and is likely to feel that she has failed once again. These could be signs that Amy has some degree of Specific Learning Difficulty (SpLD), such as Dyslexia.

> Joe, as we could see is a pupil with impulsive actions, poor concentration and a need to be constantly on the move. His behaviour did not seem to be always deliberate; rather it seemed at times that he couldn't help himself. Further investigations could well find that Joe has an attention disorder such as Attention Deficit Disorder (ADD) or Attention Deficit/Hyperactivity Disorder (AD/HD).

> Sarah was obviously unprepared for what was going to happen next and she became distressed the more attention she received. She displayed her anxiety by biting her finger and refusing to join the group. It was clear she was finding it difficult to mix with her peer group. Sarah may well be a pupil with social communication difficulties and displays behaviours which could be on the autism spectrum, often referred to as ASD.

David had fine motor difficulties which hindered all his written work. The teacher may well find that he is sometimes quite clumsy and finds other physical activities challenging. David isn't a lazy pupil and will often work much harder than his peers to compensate for his weaknesses; unfortunately, his output of work may not reflect this. His difficulties are typical of a pupil with Developmental Co-ordination Disorder or Dyspraxia.

Lucy has difficulties learning across all areas of the curriculum. She is consistently behind her peers in levels of attainment. She will need sustained adult input in order to access the curriculum. However, she is learning, but progress is very slow. She has general learning difficulties and is developmentally delayed.

Frankie is typical of a child who often gets overlooked in a class. It's a bit of a mystery; his speech is OK, and he often talks a lot, but much of the language used by the teacher is too complicated for him and he doesn't understand. Frankie has an underlying language processing difficulty and this will impact on his progress in all areas of school life.

Jordan has many difficult behaviours related to social and emotional problems. Bad behaviour should not be condoned but an understanding of the causal factors can assist us in taking the correct steps to attempt to improve it.

Annabel has an overt difficulty; she has a hearing impairment. Everyone is aware of this and is generally considerate towards her. The school receives advice and support on a regular basis from the Hearing Impairment Advisory Service.

Amy and her friends are all fictitious. What we have tried to do is describe some of the features of the various educational challenges which are evident in many mainstream classes. Wouldn't it be easy if we could fit all these children with SEN into these neat little compartments? Unfortunately, real life is never like that! Even though we have tried to give you a quick pen picture of the nature of these difficulties, in reality there is often a co-existence of several. For example, a pupil might have Visual Impairment and Autism Spectrum Disorder (ASD), Dyslexia and Dyspraxia, Learning and Language Delays, ASD and AD/HD and so the list could go on. Also, within each of the above categories it must be remembered that these are just **some** of the features presented and are by no means exclusive or exhaustive; we will look in more detail at these and other areas of SEN when we reach the next stop on our tour.

But, before we get there, let's have a look at recent research figures. It is estimated that 1 in 10 people have a language difficulty; 1 in 10 people are affected by Dyslexia and between 1 in 10 and 1 in 50 people have Dyspraxia. The prevalence rate for ASD is 91 per 10,000; and there are many other disabilities and syndromes which, when added together, mean that schools are likely to have a mixed population with approximately 20% of pupils who have some form of SEN. (Source: DfES)

Around 44,000 children and young people in Scotland have special educational needs, roughly 1 in 20 or 5.9% of the school population. Of that number, around 8,200 are educated in special schools a statistic which has remained steady for the last seven years.

(Source: School census 2001 quoted in "Moving to Mainstream" Audit Scotland & HMIE May 2003)   162,103

Therefore, the more we know and try to understand the nature and the range of their difficulties, the more we can do to help our pupils achieve their full potential. Also by recognising and identifying their difficulties, we can take advantage of past research and successful interventions and strategies that are likely to make a difference.

Chapter Five

An Overview
of Difficulties

In the next section we are going to take a look at some of the most common difficulties found in our classrooms today. This book is not intended to be a heavy and technical read; rather we want our readers to enjoy a straightforward, yet informative overview of the world of Special Educational Needs. However, we felt that it was necessary to include some detail of certain conditions and disabilities and so we have undertaken to provide readers with a brief résumé. They can be categorised under five main headings:

■ Physical and Sensory

■ General and Specific Learning Difficulties

■ Language Difficulties

■ Autism Spectrum Disorders

■ Social, Emotional and Behavioural Difficulties

Chapter Six

Physical and Sensory Difficulties

In some ways, the identification and management of pupils with a physical or sensory (i.e. visual or hearing) difficulty can be a more straightforward task than with other forms of difficulty. This is largely due to the very obvious nature of the disability.

Physical Difficulties

There are many reasons for physical disability, and this book is not intended to be a medical thesis. However, we shall mention a few types of physical difficulty which are more prevalent than others, and which the average teacher or teaching assistant may come across during the course of their career. These are:

- **Cerebral Palsy**. This describes a physical impairment that affects movement, due to a failure of development, or damage to, the part of the brain which controls movement. Cerebral Palsy occurs in approximately 1 in 400 births. (Source: Scope) The disability varies in its severity. The causes can include problems during the birthing process, extreme pre-maturity, or illness in very young infants. Sometimes infections, either during pregnancy, or in the infant or young child, can cause Cerebral Palsy. Sometimes the cause is not known. There are different types of Cerebral Palsy, all of which manifest in different ways. Children with any form can also unfortunately have other difficulties, such as sensory or learning difficulties.

- **Spina Bifida**. This condition is caused by a defect in the formation of the spine or spinal cord very early on in pregnancy which leaves a gap in the small bones of the back. Paralysis can occur below the point of defect. The severity of the condition, therefore, depends upon the position of the defect on the spine and also the extent of damage to the surrounding nerves. Approximately 80% of people with Spina Bifida also have Hydrocephalus. (Source: Asbah) The cause is as yet unknown, but the risk of Spina Bifida can be reduced by the mother taking a supplementary dose of folic acid before conception and for the first twelve weeks of pregnancy.

- **Hydrocephalus**. In this condition, there is an obstruction of the flow of Cerebro-Spinal Fluid which accumulates in the brain and causes pressure to build up. This compresses surrounding brain tissue and unfortunately can sometimes cause brain damage. Nowadays a shunt is inserted, which drains off the fluid and the child can progress in the usual way. It is important for those caring for a child with Hydrocephalus to be aware of the possible damage which can be caused if a shunt becomes blocked. School staff need to be vigilant if such a pupil shows signs of a headache, dizziness, nausea, abdominal pain, sensitivity to light or disturbed vision. If this happens, the child's parents should be contacted immediately and medical attention should be sought. (Source: Asbah)

- **Genetic syndromes**. The advances in genetic research has meant that many conditions, which previously baffled doctors, have now been identified as a genetic syndrome and named. Characteristics that are common to these syndromes have been documented, where possible treatments have been developed and support systems for those caring for children with these conditions have been set up. Probably one of the most well known genetic syndromes is, of course, Down's Syndrome, and because of the relative frequency of its occurrence in the general population it has been known for decades. Current figures indicate that Down's Syndrome occurs at the rate of 1 in every 1,000 live births. (Source: Downs Syndrome Association) In fact, it received its name after a medical paper discussing the syndrome, was published in 1866 by Dr John Langdon Down. Many more genetic syndromes, however, occur much less frequently, and so are still being newly identified today. There are so many of them, that it would never be expected of a teacher to know about even a fraction of them; however, if a pupil does have a diagnosis of any specified syndrome, the responsible teacher should access information about it via books, voluntary associations or the Internet so they can have as much knowledge as possible.

- **Accident or illness**. Frequent or prolonged illnesses take their toll on children, and if brain damage occurs as a result of an accident or illness such as meningitis, then the child may suffer physical, sensory or learning difficulties to a greater or lesser extent.

- **Medical problems**. Children who have a medical condition such as epilepsy, depression, diabetes, asthma or any other, need careful monitoring at all times for both their physical well being and also their educational progress. This may be affected by their illness or by the medication they require for treatment.

As we have seen above, many pupils with a physical disability will have had the difficulty from birth; they will have received a medical diagnosis at an early age, and often by the time they come to school at five years old their progress will have already been well supervised and documented by medics, health visitors, therapists and pre-school advisors. Their parents will be only too aware of the nature of their child's problems and have some indication of prognosis for the future. Therefore, for the school, there will not be the task of identification; also there will be programmes of therapy already in place which the school need only continue under the direction of the therapist.

Saying this does not minimise, however, the challenge that a child with a physical disability may present a school, the teachers, the other pupils and their parents and also, unfortunate but true, the school budget. The provision of a safe, comfortable and accessible environment is essential for a pupil with a physical disability, and one which the LEA, together with the school must take seriously. There should be adequate provision of facilities to meet the physical needs of the pupil, and space, together with human resources, to deliver the necessary therapy programmes on a regular basis. There might be the need to purchase specialist equipment and technology so that the pupil can access the curriculum, for example, specially designed hard and software to aid him record his work. Adaptations to the building might need to be carried out before the pupil joins the school, for example, automatic doors, safety features and so on. Most LEAs will have staff available to help schools carry out risk assessments and will be able to give advice on such matters.

Hopefully, if a pupil's difficulties are purely physical, and they are well supported by external agencies, the school might find that educating this particular type of pupil is straightforward rather than confusing, and can be an extremely positive experience for all concerned.

Sensory Difficulties

Like physical difficulties, sensory difficulties, that is, visual impairment and hearing impairment, are often apparent from birth or early childhood. They are diagnosed by a member of the medical profession, and again are likely to be well documented by the time a child reaches school age. Schools may need to budget for adaptations to the school or learning environment, for example, installing loop systems for hearing aid users or buying CCTV equipment for the magnification of print or educational artefacts for the visually impaired pupil. Staff may need to be trained in the use of sign language or Braille.

Most LEAs will have a network of specialist teachers trained to a high level to educate pupils with sensory difficulties. They will also train and advise school staff on good practice for working with these pupils.

Again like physical difficulties, there is a large range of sensory difficulties, with diverse causes.

Chapter Seven

Learning Difficulties

General Learning Difficulties

But let us move on and visit some areas of disability which are not always quite as obvious as those mentioned above. These include a wide range of learning difficulties. Most learning difficulties cannot be objectively identified, diagnosed or medically proven, unless, as we have already seen, it accompanies a genetic syndrome or physical disability. They become evident only as time passes and the child or pupil fails to reach expected developmental or academic milestones. They are identifiable primarily through the observation and assessment of the pupil by parents, carers, teachers and other interested adults. The early identification of learning difficulties, particularly those of a moderate or mild nature, is notoriously tricky because all children, especially young ones, grow, develop and learn at widely varying rates. For example, children start to talk within a window of time which can begin as early as 12 to 18 months or as late as 30 months. Therefore, they can arrive in the Nursery or Reception Class with widely differing competencies and abilities, yet still be within the 'norm' for their age group. No one should be keen to jump to what could be erroneous conclusions about a young child. Rather, it is better to do all one can to stimulate his development and wait to see if increased maturity helps rectify the situation. It is also extremely worrying for a parent to be told that a professional suspects their child of having a learning difficulty, and if this proves to be untrue over time, it could be seen to have been a mistaken professional judgement and to have caused unnecessary anxiety to the parents.

However, if a teacher becomes aware that a young pupil in her class seems to be developing more slowly than the other pupils, she will be wise to provide additional input and support for him immediately, and closely monitor his progress. She might be well advised to discuss this with the parents and work closely with them to maximise his potential at home as well as at school.

It is in the light of the increased challenges and pace of the academic curriculum of course, as the child gets older, that any learning difficulties will become more evident. For example, a pupil may experience problems grasping basic phonic work in Literacy, or the concept of number in Numeracy. Difficulties at this stage with these early skills can be disastrous, as much of the rest of the curriculum taught higher up the school system is founded upon an efficient use of literacy and numeracy. For example, history, geography, and RE, are subjects which rely heavily on written recorded work; likewise, the sciences, technology and to some extent geography and music lean on basic numeracy skills for success. Needless to say, the government, schools, and teachers everywhere are only too aware of this, which is why there is such an emphasis on Literacy and Numeracy and why a corresponding amount of funding, time and resources from the top down are ploughed into promoting them and remedying them where necessary.

Ultimately, however, the responsibility for identifying a learning difficulty in the first instance lies firmly with the class teacher and Special Educational Needs Co-ordinator (SENCo) of the school. In Scotland this would be done by the class teacher in collaboration with the Support for Learning teacher (SfL). They are the ones at the 'chalk face'; they are the ones who know their pupils better than anyone else, and it is their vigilance, helped by the observation skills of a knowledgeable teaching assistant, which can put wheels into motion early on which will only benefit that pupil.

Suspicion is aroused when a pupil consistently fails to make a similar amount of progress as his or her peers. A good teacher will in the first instance support the pupil, either by themselves or through the help of a teaching assistant, and ensure that work tasks are suitably differentiated for them, so that they can experience success and their self esteem is protected. However, if difficulties persist, it may be the time to discuss the pupil's progress with the school SENCo or SfL teacher. She is likely to look at the pupil's work, observe him working in class and maybe do some simple standardised assessments with him. Standardised assessments give a comparison between the pupil's achievement or performance and the national average for children of that particular age. This will help to clarify the severity of the difficulty and help the school prioritise action and support for the pupil. From these investigations, the school may either feel confident to tackle the problems themselves, or may prefer to refer the case on to external professionals who will advise further.

Top tips: Learning difficulties

- Ensure the language you use is at the level the pupil can understand
- Reinforce auditory teaching with visual aids to maximise understanding
- Be explicit with instructions and keep them succinct
- Allow time for responding to and processing information
- Remember to differentiate all tasks so that the pupil can experience success
- Break tasks down into small steps
- Plan time for practice and over learning of new skills
- Have realistic expectations; however this is not the same as low expectations
- Build on any strengths that the pupil may have to maintain good self esteem
- Give plenty of encouragement and praise good effort!

However, as research into the nature of learning difficulties has advanced, a distinction has emerged between what has become known as 'general learning difficulties' and others known as 'specific learning difficulties'. While at first sight these two categories display similar outward effects on learning, the underlying causes are quite distinct and require a different approach to remediation. Therefore it is more than just desirable; one could say it is essential, for the correct identification of the difficulty to be made.

A pupil who has a general learning difficulty is likely to display developmental and learning delay right across the range of subjects and areas of school life. That is to say that he will probably find numeracy as difficult as he finds literacy; he may well find listening and understanding language hard and will consequently have a lower level of expressive language. Keeping up with the pace of the rest of the class, i.e. following management instructions and organising himself may also be a challenge. On the whole, you could describe such a pupil as having an even profile of ability, but one which is behind his peers in every area.

Specific Learning Difficulties

On the other hand, let's take a look at the pupil who you suspect may have specific learning difficulties. His profile of ability, which we have just mentioned above, is rather more uneven. He may well be within the average or even above average range for his age when it comes to maths, technology or science, for example, yet he is performing significantly below the average level for pupils of his age in literacy. Persistent underperformance in reading and writing does not seem compatible with his achievements in other areas of the curriculum. The teacher may well question why it is that he does so poorly in some areas when he is clearly an able pupil in other areas. It is precisely this inconsistency which may alert the teacher to the possibility of a specific learning difficulty and which should provoke further investigation. Again, discussion with the school SENCo or SfL teacher is the first step to take, after which screenings for specific learning difficulties might be arranged. These can sometimes be carried out by the SENCo or SfL teacher; otherwise the pupil may need to be referred to an external professional.

Dyslexia

Specific learning difficulties have been a lively subject of debate over the past few decades. The most well known and well researched one is, of course, Dyslexia. In fact, symptoms of Dyslexia were first documented way back in the nineteenth century, when it was called 'word blindness'. It accompanied the observation of otherwise seemingly bright pupils who persisted in failing at basic reading, spelling and writing. With progress in the field of genetics, it is now fairly certain that many cases of Dyslexia are inherited; very often there is a history of the difficulty in the family and statistically we know that three times as many males are dyslexic as females (CAF Directory). Current figures estimate that as many as 10% of the population have some form of Dyslexia, with 4% being severely affected. (Source: The Dyslexia Institute)

As teachers and teaching assistants, we need to watch keenly for signs of possible Dyslexia.

Look out for: Dyslexia

- Poor and dysfluent reading
- Persistently poor spelling
- Poor working memory
- Possible good cognitive abilities in other areas
- Pupil tries hard and tires easily
- Pupil may have had early oral language problems
- Family history
- Pupil may have poor laterality, i.e. they may not have a dominant eye or hand

Recent research has highlighted the correlation between early phonological awareness and later literacy skills. Phonological awareness is having the ability to hear differences between sounds, identify them, blend them, hear syllables and break words up into parts, hear rhyme and generally be able to play around with words orally. If a young child can do this efficiently, then he will more easily be able to do the same with the written word. If he cannot do this, it is likely to hinder his reading, spelling and writing. A diligent and knowledgeable Early Years or Key Stage 1 teacher might be able to spot a weakness early on and put the pupil onto a programme to enrich phonological skills.

There are a number of commercialised diagnostic tests available nowadays to screen for Dyslexia. Some schools will have a trained member of staff able to use such a test, while other schools will need to refer to an outside specialist teacher or psychologist to help with this. Firm confirmation of Dyslexia will help a pupil as they go through their education as it can mean time concessions in written tests and public examinations. These concessions could make all the difference to a pupil taking an examination which relies heavily on the recorded written word. In severe cases an amanuensis, or scribe, may be permitted to record information for the pupil.

The pupil may also find the actual printed word difficult to see and read, which could indicate further complications such as Irlen Syndrome. This is also known as Scotopic Sensitivity Syndrome and is a visual processing difficulty. It is suggested from the research that as many as 40% of people who are Dyslexic may also have Irlen Syndrome. Fortunately, this condition is relatively straightforward to treat by the use of coloured plastic overlays on the printed page, or by the wearing of coloured filters in spectacles; so where Dyslexia is diagnosed, it may be wise to screen the pupil for Irlen Syndrome as well.

A very structured approach to the teaching of reading and spelling has been found to be useful in helping pupils with Dyslexia. There are a number of literacy programmes on the market where phonics are taught in a steady and methodical way (synthetic phonics). These usually require adult input and are therefore demanding in terms of human resources. However, there are often pupils who would benefit from such a programme and groups could be formed to work together. As the pupil progresses up the school, he should be allowed to make the best possible use of ICT so that his achievement in other subjects is not disadvantaged by his lack of literacy skills.

Top tips: Dyslexia

- Check that the pupil is secure with their knowledge of phonics, e.g. letter sounds, digraphs (i.e. a pair of letters that represent a single sound), etc.

- Re-visit any gaps

- Allow plenty of time for practising phonic skills

- Look for a good, structured programme; there are many on the market

- Practise memory skills

- Use a multi-sensory approach, i.e. teach through all the senses

- When practising spellings, try the 'Look, say, copy, cover, write and check' method

- Remember that pupils with dyslexia may tire quickly and be careful not to overload with homework

- For older pupils allow alternative methods of recording their work, e.g. computer, Dictaphone™

- Keep self esteem healthy by building on areas of strength and praising effort

Dyspraxia

Another specific learning difficulty that has become well known more recently is Dyspraxia. This is also known by a number of other names, e.g. Developmental Co-ordination Disorder, Perceptuo-Motor Dysfunction, and, more colloquially, 'Clumsy Child Syndrome'. This last one gives us a clue as to the main characteristics of this disorder, namely, an impairment of motor function which causes poor co-ordination of movement. However, the cause of this motor impairment is not due to a medical condition such as the ones described under our section on Physical

Disability, nor is it due to damage or weakness to nerves or muscles. Rather it is a difficulty with the processing and controlling of movements. Again, Dyspraxia may be mild or severe and, like Dyslexia, it affects more males than females. It is estimated that approximately 10% of the population have Dyspraxia, with 2% being severely affected. Four times as many males as females are affected. (Source: The Dyspraxia Foundation)

Diagnosis is usually through a member of the medical profession; Doctor, Occupational Therapist, Physiotherapist or sometimes an Educational Psychologist.

Most dyspraxic pupils have average cognitive abilities and typically they have better verbal than visual skills. They usually find sequencing, organisation and planning very hard and they can often struggle with maths. Above all, however, a pupil's difficulties will be most evident in their handwriting. Neat handwriting will be elusive for the pupil and this will hinder the output of written work.

All this usually translates into an uneven profile of academic ability. It has been noted also that there is an increased chance of behavioural difficulties in a pupil with Dyspraxia.

A teacher or teaching assistant can identify a pupil who may have Dyspraxia through watching for certain signs.

Look out for: Dyspraxia

- Delays in physical milestones or speech
- Difficulty with self help skills such as dressing and undressing
- Dropping and knocking things over frequently
- Tripping up too often
- Poor performance in sport and poor awareness of own body movements
- Poor handwriting

They will not be able to diagnose the condition, but they may be able to discuss their observations with the parents who might agree to take their child to visit their GP for further investigations.

Pupils with Dyspraxia can be helped by teachers ensuring a good seating position (often improved by the use of a specially designed chair), and by the use of specialist writing pens and pencils. There are a number of pencil grips and ergonomically designed pens available from suppliers of special needs equipment which can make a big improvement to a pupil's handwriting. A writing slope placed on the desktop will also help his writing posture and is not expensive to buy. None of this equipment is expensive and can be used again for future pupils. Of course, as the pupil gets older, he should be allowed to record his written work on a computer whenever possible.

Top tips: Dyspraxia

- Make sure the pupil has a correct seated posture when writing, i.e. with the bottom in the back of the seat and the feet flat on the floor

- Explore using a range of writing implements to see which one the pupil prefers

- Be aware that handwriting is often very hard work, and their hands may feel tired quickly

- Acknowledge their best work, even if it is untidy

- Make good use of the computer or Dictaphone™ to record work

- Remember that low volume of work does not necessarily equal laziness

- Be sympathetic with the pupil in PE as they are likely to find all areas of this subject difficult, especially changing

- Encourage sympathetic awareness from peers

- If the pupil has an occupational therapy programme, ensure it is carried out

- Maintain self esteem by building on his strengths

Dyscalculia

A third difficulty, which is included in the category of specific learning difficulties, is another word which begins with the prefix 'dys' (which comes from Greek and indicates something abnormal). This is Dyscalculia, and a very simplistic way of describing it is to liken it to Dyslexia, but applying it to mathematics instead. The study of Dyscalculia has reached the stage the study of Dyslexia was approximately 10 or 15 years ago. It is only now being recognised as a specific learning difficulty and one hypothesis is that somehow the innate capacity for number is lacking. However true that may be, a pupil with Dyscalculia has a mathematical ability which is substantially below what you would expect him to achieve given his chronological age and cognitive abilities shown in other areas of the curriculum.

Look out for: Dyscalculia

■ Difficulties with numbers – symbol reversal, confusion between digits, errors when reading or copying two or more digits

■ Difficulties with the value of number – understanding the 'oneness' of one, e.g. that one ant has the same value as one aeroplane; difficulties with place value

■ Difficulties understanding the 'four operations' – addition, subtraction, multiplication, division; difficulties with the meaning of the symbols + – x ÷ and problems with language relating to symbols

■ Poor knowledge of number facts, for example, times tables

■ Difficulties remembering sequences and formulas

■ Difficulties with mental maths

As with Dyslexia, poor working memory plays an important part in Dyscalculia. The pupil may find it hard to shift between types of arithmetic, so a careful teacher will avoid giving different types of calculations in the same session. The pupil may find spatial tasks a problem, e.g. North, South, East, and West, horizontal and vertical, and left/right orientation. All these could have some impact on other subjects such as geography or technology when he is asked to do tasks such as read maps, interpret graphical data, or play a musical instrument.

Top tips: Dyscalculia

- Teach and practise one type of calculation at a time
- Only teach one new fact per lesson
- Always teach progressively, building new and harder skills upon secure, easier ones.
- Provide plenty of practice to retain information
- Teach in a multi-sensory way, i.e. through all senses
- Give pupils extra time to work things out
- Use squared paper to help pupils keep their number columns correct
- Always praise effort to help keep self esteem high

Chapter Eight

Speech and Language Difficulties

'The limits of my language are the limits of my world.'

Wittgenstein

Although people have been using language to communicate since the dawn of time, research continues to try and ascertain exactly how language is acquired and what has happened when it goes wrong. The study of speech and language is a vast and specialised area and Speech and Language Therapy is a profession in its own right. Therapists are highly skilled and knowledgeable and their expertise is vital in helping teaching staff identify and address speech and language difficulties which may well be a contributory factor to other educational needs. So many pupils with a special educational need have associated speech, language and communication difficulties.

It is important at this point to emphasise that there is a difference between *speech* and *language*, although there is sometimes a link between the two. Put very simply, language is the internal, mental process of using a system and structure to communicate with others. There are many alternative forms of communication which do not involve speech, e.g. signing, Braille, gesture etc. Speech is the outward and audible expression of that language using our voices.

Language is a two-way process involving receptive language, i.e. the receiving and understanding of words and phrases used, and expressive language, which involves formulating your thoughts in the form of words and sentences and conveying them using the semantic and grammatical rules of language. The understanding of a language comes before we are able to use it expressively. Just consider how we learn a foreign language, where we can pick up the gist of a conversation long before we can contribute to it, or the very young child who can understand far more than they can say.

As we have said, many pupils with SEN might have a language difficulty which could be either a language delay or a specific language impairment or disorder.

A delay implies the pupil's language is following the typical pattern of development, but at a much slower rate than expected for their chronological age. A specific language impairment or disorder means that the pattern of development is uneven and atypical. The definite identification of either an impairment or a disorder requires the expertise of a speech and language therapist.

Children acquire their language at different rates, but the average child will go through the following developmental stages:

The chart below has been taken from 'I CAN' and represents typical language development and what a typical child will be doing. However, it must be remembered that there is a wide range within development and this is to be used as a guide only.

Age of Child	Typical Language Development
3–4 years	• Listening to longer stories than before
	• Understanding and often using colour, number and time related words, for example, 'red' car, 'three' fingers and 'yesterday/tomorrow'
	• Using longer sentences and linking these sentences together
	• Describing events that have already happened – 'we went to the park'
	• Enjoying make believe play
	• Starting to like simple jokes
	• Continuing to ask many questions

Age of Child	Typical Language Development
3–4 years (continued)	• Still making mistakes with tense, for example saying 'runned' for ran and 'swimmed' for swam
	• Having a few difficulties with a small number of sounds – for example r/w/l,f/th and s/sh/ch/dz
4–5 years	• Able to understand spoken instructions related to an activity without stopping what they are doing to look at the speaker
	• Choosing their own friends and playmates
	• Taking turns in much longer conversations
	• Understanding more complicated language (e.g. first, last, might, may be, above and in between)
	• Using sentences that are well formed. They may still have some difficulties with grammar (e.g. with some plurals like saying 'sheeps' instead of 'sheep' or more complicated tenses like using 'goed' instead of 'went')
	• Thinking more about the meaning of words – perhaps describing what simple words mean or asking what a new word means when they first hear it
	• Using most sounds effectively – perhaps having some difficulties with words with lots of syllables or consonant sounds close together for example 'scribble' or 'elephant'
	• Remain focused on one activity for increasing lengths of time without being reminded to do so
5 years onwards	• Continue to learn new words. Their vocabulary will increase enormously. Especially with words learnt at school. As children get older, they rely less on pictures and objects to learn new language, and so are able to learn simply through hearing and reading new words. However, using visual materials helps older children and even adults to learn new words
	• Use their language skills in learning to read, write and spell
	• Learn that the same word can mean two things, e.g. 'orange' the fruit and 'orange' the colour

Age of Child	Typical Language Development
5 years onwards (continued)	• Learn that different words can mean the same thing, e.g. minus and take away
	• Understand concepts and ideas that are abstract – like feelings and descriptive words, e.g. 'carefully', 'slowly' or 'clever'
	• Use language for different purposes, e.g. to persuade, negotiate or question
	• Share and discuss, more complex and abstract ideas, like relationships, with others
	• Use language to predict and draw conclusions
	• Use language effectively in a range of different social situations
	• Understand more complicated humour and figurative language (like sarcasm)

These developmental stages have been provided by Talking Point, www.talkingpoint.org.uk, a very useful website about speech and language difficulties in children.

When it all Goes Wrong

Speech

It is relatively easy for all of us to identify a speech problem. This is the inability to articulate sounds and words correctly and speak clearly. We will usually find it difficult to understand what pupils with such a difficulty are saying. Reasons for this can be many and varied, but can include:

- a physical dysfunction inside the mouth, e.g. a cleft palate

- oral or verbal dypraxia where, like motor dyspraxia, there is a problem with processing information from the brain. The pupil with oral dyspraxia will have difficulty controlling the speech sound system, which is the mouth, tongue, lips and jaw in order for them to utter the correct sounds and sequence of sounds for speech. There is usually nothing wrong with the muscles themselves and the pupil is usually quite able to perform other oro-motor movements such as chewing, swallowing and coughing. Basically, the area of the brain which tells the muscles what to do to produce sounds and sequences of sounds is either underdeveloped or damaged.

- Associated hearing loss where certain sounds cannot be accurately imitated.

Language
It is a much harder task to identify a language problem because of the 'hidden nature' of it.

Remembering that this is merely a Whistle-Stop Tour, for the purpose of this book we are going to discuss the following topics which in our experience are ones which we have most frequently encountered in schools:

- Comprehension difficulties
- Inadequate vocabulary and word finding difficulties
- Semantic difficulties
- Pragmatic difficulties

Comprehension or receptive difficulties
Comprehension in its simplest form means understanding, but in the context of language includes the whole area of semantics, i.e. grammatical structure, vocabulary and word meaning. The implications of a comprehension difficulty are enormous in school. If a pupil cannot understand what is being taught through a teacher's words, then this will have a serious impact on their long-term learning. You cannot use what you have not understood. Therefore, some pupils may gain little from whole class teaching which is delivered through the spoken word. And, as literacy is a written form of the spoken word, we can easily see how if there is a language delay or disorder, then there is likely to be accompanying problems with literacy.

Look out for: Receptive difficulties

- Inability to follow instructions
- Poor recall of what has been said
- Signs of mistaken understanding
- Reduced use of vocabulary
- Misunderstanding of question words (what, why, where, who and when)
- Associated poor expressive use of language

Inadequate vocabulary and word finding difficulties

The normally developing child will have acquired a vocabulary of approximately 50 to 200 words by the age of two years old. By five, they will know 2,000 to 5,000 words and by the age of ten they will know 8,000 to 10,000 words. Remember that the term 'vocabulary' is more than just nouns; it includes verbs, adjectives, prepositions, adverbs, and so on. The word finding process involves understanding what the word means, being able to remember a large number of different words, and storing them efficiently so we can find the word again when required. The way we store them seems to be important for retrieval, and we do this by creating links such as semantic links. These are groupings of words which are linked together by classification or meaning.

Look out for: Word problems

- Impoverished vocabulary
- Use of words such as 'thingy', 'wotsit'
- Over use of gesture to replace words
- 'It's on the tip of my tongue' … they know the word but can't access it

Semantic difficulties

As previously mentioned a semantic competence requires the ability to understand and use the structures of language, i.e. grammatical rules, word, phrase and sentence meanings. In addition it covers the whole area of figurative language, including the understanding of idioms and other non-literal language. When one stops to actually analyse our own use of language, we might be surprised at how often we don't say what we really mean, nor do we mean what we say! For example, 'Just you do that one more time...!'

Look out for: Semantic difficulties

- Difficulty understanding the meaning of words, phrases and sentences
- Difficulties understanding abstract concepts
- Difficulty with extracting overall meaning from language
- A tendency to apply a literal interpretation to language; failure to understand the use of figurative language, idioms (e.g. 'I've got a frog in my throat'), metaphors, implied meanings, inference, sarcasm
- Not recognising or understanding intonation or emphasis within a sentence
- A tendency to use language through memorizing and rote learning
- Confused use of grammar, e.g. wrong word order, wrong use of words and tenses

Pragmatic difficulties

Pragmatics refers to the use of language in a social context. Basically, knowing what to say, how to say it and when to say it. At a fundamental level it is how we use our language to interact and communicate with others. It is knowing that we behave and speak differently to different kinds of people, e.g. your mum and your Head Teacher. It is understanding the natural give and take of a conversation, giving and receiving eye contact, taking turns and knowing when to speak and when to listen. It is also the ability to interpret others' non-verbal use of language, i.e. posture, gestures, facial expressions.

Pupils often have a combination of these two difficulties although they can occur separately. In addition, there is a strong link between the occurrence of these two difficulties, particularly pragmatics, with an Autism Spectrum Disorder. Pupils can receive a diagnosis of Semantic Disorder or Pragmatic Disorder, or a Semantic Pragmatic Disorder. Younger pupils with ASD are likely to have problems with both semantics and pragmatics and it is not unusual for a pragmatic difficulty to continue into later life. Therefore, by definition we can see that this becomes not only a language problem, but a wider general communication difficulty.

Look out for: Pragmatic difficulties

- Inappropriate use of language in social situations
- Poor conversation skills, e.g. poor turn taking, interrupting
- Unawareness of their own inappropriate comments
- Lack of understanding that comments deemed to be rude can hurt other people's feelings
- A tendency to be ruthlessly honest!
- A lack of understanding of non-verbal language

If we return to our fictitious pupil, Frankie, who we met earlier on, we can see that he had no particular difficulty with the articulation of sounds and words; in fact he was happy to talk a lot! However, Frankie has a difficulty with his understanding of language, which has a two-fold effect; firstly, he finds it hard to understand and follow what is being said, and secondly his own use of language is likely to be restricted which could lead to a sense of frustration in his ability to express himself. This might also affect his socialisation skills and the development of friendships.

Even if a school has only limited access to a Speech and Language Therapy Service, there is still a significant amount that teachers and teaching assistants can do to develop and improve a pupil's language ability.

First of all, check the points listed above to see if any of them apply to your pupil. Confer with other adults who work with the pupil. If a language difficulty is suspected, there are a number of commercially produced assessments and checklists which can be used by teachers to confirm and identify the nature and extent of the difficulty. A quick phone call to your school's Speech and Language Therapist will inform you of the ones that teachers can administer and would be most suitable for your pupil.

Armed with this knowledge, you are in a better position to adapt your own delivery of language to suit the needs of the pupil. You can more skilfully select and adapt suitable programmes, activities and resources that would be of most benefit to him.

On the next page are some top tips for working with a pupil who has been formally identified or you have identified as having a language difficulty.

Top tips: Language difficulties

- Use an appropriate level of language (be clear and concise)

- Regularly check for understanding during lessons

- Make good and specific use of other adults in class; they can often provide an interface between the class teacher and the pupil

- Avoid constant correction of poor use of language, e.g. incorrect tenses

- Model good use of language

- Wherever possible allow time for talking

- Teach new and unfamiliar vocabulary before topics begin

- Back up oral teaching with as much visual information as possible; i.e. pictures, objects, symbols etc.

- Make the best possible use of your own body language

- Be aware of non-literal language you are using in class, and be prepared to give an explanation where necessary

- Consider giving specific language teaching through small group work, e.g. conceptual language (in, on, under), using language appropriately, increasing vocabulary

Chapter Nine

Autism
Spectrum Disorder (ASD)

As approximately 500,000 families in the UK are affected by autism (Source: NAS), it is highly likely that you will be working with or supporting a pupil who has a diagnosis of an Autism Spectrum Disorder.

Where did it all Begin?

Leo Kanner, a child psychologist back in 1943, was the first person to describe and name a pattern of behaviour he observed in a small group of boys. A year later, Austrian psychologist Hans Asperger, quite unaware of Kanner's findings was also observing and reporting on older children with very similar behavioural traits, although he found they had no real language delay but tended to be quite bright. He also noticed that they were disorganised and at times clumsy. He used the term 'autistic' in relation to the behaviour he saw. His work was in German and was not translated until the early eighties, when the term Asperger Syndrome was first used by Lorna Wing, but it has only been included in the diagnostic manuals for the last decade.

What is ASD?

Definitions of ASD change frequently as research unveils more findings and provides us with more information, but basically people with an autism spectrum disorder find many social aspects difficult. In addition they tend to be rather rigid and inflexible in everyday life; they like routines and predictability. It is a developmental disorder which means that the nature of people's difficulties and strengths change with time.

Children and adults with ASD vary in their intellectual abilities. This ranges from severely disabled up to those people who have very superior skills or intelligence. There are some people who have outstanding 'savant skills' such as the artist Stephen Wiltshire.

An ASD is not curable but with appropriate early intervention, support and education, a child can be helped to maximise their skills and achieve their full potential as adults.

All the Different Names!

In schools you may find a variety of terminology used on various reports and by different professionals. These may include:

- Autistic Spectrum Disorder
- Autism
- Asperger Syndrome
- Pervasive Developmental Disorder
- Social and Communication Disorder
- Autistic tendencies
- Autistic traits

At present it is generally agreed that all the above fall under the umbrella of Autism Spectrum Disorder and this term can be used describe people who present with profound difficulties to those who appear to have mild difficulties.

How is a Diagnosis Made and who Makes it?

Specific criteria are used to make a diagnosis and to receive a diagnosis a person has to have impairment in the following three areas:

- Social interaction
- Social communication
- Inflexibility of thought and behaviour

These are known as the 'Triad of Impairments', a term that was first used by Lorna Wing in the early eighties.

Although Asperger Syndrome is considered to fall within the spectrum, it has enough distinct features to warrant a label of its own. A diagnosis of Asperger Syndrome is mostly given when there is no real language delay or there has not been a marked delay at an early age and cognitive functioning (ability) is above average. In addition, difficulties with gross (whole body movements) or fine motor (hand and arm movements) skills are taken into consideration when making the assessment.

A diagnosis is usually made by the medical profession; a paediatrician, or clinical psychologist. It is not the role of staff in schools to make a diagnosis but to highlight the difficulty and make the correct referrals.

How Might they Behave?

Just as no two children are the same, they are individuals, so our pupils with ASD cannot be judged as all functioning and behaving in the same manner. However, they do have difficulties that are often similar.

Let's look at the different parts of the Triad:

Social Interaction

Children with ASD can find the whole social 'etiquette' an impossible task. Who taught you 'how to be with other people'? In truth the answer is probably no one, you may have had to be told how to speak to someone, how to behave and had the occasional reminders but on the whole it was something you learnt almost innately. At this point it is important to remember that for many people with ASD many social and communication skills are not learnt innately; they have to be taught, and often re-taught … many times!

Some pupils prefer to withdraw from a lot of social contact and avoid social situations whilst others do want to be accepted by their peers but often lack the skills needed for successful interaction. Often their behaviours are described as odd, as they may display inappropriate ways of greeting, e.g. using language inappropriately or touching others' clothes etc. They may not understand that different social situations may require different social behaviours and consequently sometimes they may appear antisocial and aggressive.

Social Communication

Many people with ASD never develop speech or use it as a means for communication. Some children have very good expressive language, but may have difficulty expressing meanings, as they often interpret information and language literally. So saying 'Do you want to read with me?' or 'You do that again' may not elicit the responses you were expecting! Furthermore their difficulties in communication can extend to not understanding the complex area of non-verbal language. Because of their inability to interpret these cues they miss the point of what is being said or what they are asked to do.

Let's take a conversation as an example and examine the skills necessary for successful interaction. Firstly, it takes two people, then you begin talking about a certain topic. From thereon:

- You listen whilst the other person is talking
- You appear interested in what the other person is saying (even though you may not be)
- You make appropriate responses
- You take turns
- You learn how to repair a conversation when it goes wrong
- You make judgements from the other person's body language, facial expressions, intonation, as to how interested or disinterested they are
- You know when to change the topic.

A person with ASD will find some or all of these skills difficult because they:

- May only want to talk about their chosen topic

- Interrupt often as they misunderstand the idea about taking turns

- Appear bored or disinterested sometimes to the point of walking away

- Appear rude because they have a knack of being very honest without the understanding that some things are best thought, not said

- May not understand the intonation being used by the speaker and similarly fails to interpret the metaphors, idioms and figures of speech

- May not understand the whole area of non-verbal language, they may fail to pick up the cues of facial expressions and body language.

So it is not hard to understand that if a person has most of the above difficulties, social situations and interacting with others on a social level is not going to be a particularly easy task. Noting the above behaviours, the link between ASD and pragmatic difficulties becomes apparent.

Inflexibility of Thought and Behaviour

In a young child impairment with play and imaginative activities is noticeable. They do not tend to play or join in with their peers in the usual imaginative games. They can be fixated on specific toys or objects, preferring to play with them rather than with other children. They prefer routines and an environment which is predictable and often changes in the routine can cause stress and anxiety. They want, and have a need for sameness, often not wanting to try any thing different. Their repetitive and obsessive behaviours can dominate daily activities; for example taking the same route in the car, and eating the same food for lunch each day. However, as ASD is a developmental disorder, the nature of the difficulties may change over time but it is not unusual to have one obsession or subject of particular interest to be replaced by another one.

'Mind Reading'

As human beings, we can all 'mind read' or have what is known as a 'Theory of Mind'. That is, we have the ability, to some degree or another, to understand what another person is thinking. For example, if I am delayed for a lunch appointment with my friend, I can be pretty certain that she is worrying about where I am and hoping I haven't either forgotten or had an accident of some kind to prevent me being there.

This ability to understand the thoughts of others, this ability to 'mind read', develops typically in a child at around four years of age. They begin to understand that other people have thoughts, knowledge, beliefs and desires that are different from their own. They also realise that these thoughts will have an influence on them and their behaviours. 'If I throw my juice on the floor, then Mummy will be cross and I might be in trouble'.

People with Autism Spectrum Disorders find it difficult to conceptualise or appreciate the thoughts and feelings of another person. This is why such people may talk incessantly 'at' you about their favourite topic, for example, trains or computer games. They might also assume that you know what they already know, even when it would be obvious that you wouldn't.

The following is an easy and simple test, which is sometimes used by professionals to assess whether a child has developed the ability to mind read.

'The Sally-Anne Test'

Here, the adult has two dolls, one named Sally and the other named Anne. There is a box and a basket (each covered with a cloth), and a marble. The child watches while Sally places the marble in the box and covers it over with the cloth. Sally now leaves the room. While Sally is away, Anne takes the marble out of the box and transfers it to the basket, covering it over with the cloth. Sally returns. The child is asked, 'Where will Sally look for the marble?' The typically developing child will immediately say, 'In the box'. The child with ASD will say, 'In the basket'. The reasoning seems to be, that if I know, then others should also know.

Theory of mind can develop in a child with ASD, but usually does so at a much later age, often well into the teenage years. In some people with ASD, it never completely develops.

Central Coherence Deficit

Central Coherence can be said to be the ability of an individual to draw together parts in order to construct a whole, and to make sense out of it. People with ASD have difficulties with this type of processing and often concentrate or focus on the detail of things rather than seeing or understanding the big picture.

For example, a teacher may be sharing a story book about a runaway train, and the child with ASD seems only interested and indeed fixated on the number of shiny wheels the train has, or possibly the number of spokes on each wheel. He seems completely unaware of the overall gist of the story or of any consequences for the poor passengers on board the train.

These observations were confirmed by research which took place in the late 1980s. It showed that children with ASD scored much more highly than expected on tests where attention to detail, figure/ground discrimination (e.g. 'Where's Wally?' books), and visual perception tasks were involved. It was concluded that the advantage that children with ASD had in these tests was their tendency to see the parts rather than the whole picture.

The implications of Central Coherence Deficit on pupils' social competence may be significant. In addition, they may become easily de-motivated if they cannot see the big picture of where they are going or why they are doing things.

Other Factors that May have Implications in School

Many children and adults with ASD have sensory and perceptual differences that may affect them and these can have an impact on their functioning in school. For some children certain noises can cause discomfort and they may also have auditory processing difficulties; that is, a problem interpreting aural messages. Others may be distracted by too much visual information, while there are those that can find certain materials uncomfortable to touch or wear. Many young children will eat only certain food as they do not like to try foods with differing textures. Each child will be different but it is worth remembering that many can be **hypersensitive** (excessively sensitive) to all the above while others may be **hyposensitive** (under sensitive), that is they may use noise, movement, etc. to create their own distractions, which may be at a time when they feel anxious or stressed.

Poor sequencing, understanding of time and organisational skills are another feature which also impacts on pupils. If pupils are frequently asking about what is happening, how long something lasts and what is going to happen next, then it is highly likely they haven't developed the skills to work out the order and the time it will take. For many pupils, getting themselves organised with the correct equipment at the correct time in the correct place is a hard task. These three areas can all be helped by the use of visual supports.

Being able to generalise skills learnt and use and apply them in different situations can also be an area of difficulty. It is not unusual for pupils to compartmentalise their learning and therefore it is important for us to help 'link' their learning together by relating it to concrete situations so they can try to understand the relevance of what they have learnt.

By reading the above one can begin to have the feeling that there are so many difficulties for these pupils to endure. In many cases there are, it must not be forgotten however, that there are those who have certain strengths and skills, are highly successful academically and can find meaningful employment as adults.

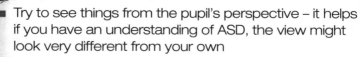

Top tips: Autism Spectrum Disorder

- Try to see things from the pupil's perspective – it helps if you have an understanding of ASD, the view might look very different from your own

- Create an orderly, structured environment and consistent environment

- Use visual supports, e.g. timetables, written information, visual organisers, Mind Maps, Social Stories

- Forewarn the pupils of any change

- Be aware of the need to generalise skills

- Be aware of a pupil's heightened sensory awareness

- Say what you mean and mean what you say, idioms, metaphors etc. will have to be taught

- Check a pupil's understanding of each situation

- Provide a quiet area to de-stress; allow for solitariness when needed

- Use the pupil's name first when addressing him

- Give them time to process and respond

- Social skills and conversation skills may need explicit teaching, preferably in context

- Explicitly address the issues of lack of self awareness

- Teach, where possible, through practical demonstration and modelling. Expect difficulties if you ask a pupil to talk or write about a situation that they have not experienced

- Be aware that homework may be a major source of tension for these pupils and their carers

- Develop good communication with carers and listen to them

- Be patient

Tourette's Syndrome

One in 100 children in our schools have Tourette's Syndrome or Tourette Syndrome as it is also known, and although many of these pupils will have associated difficulties and their education may be in a more specialist provision, there will be some who are attending mainstream schools. Therefore, we felt it was important to discuss this here.

Tourette's syndrome is an inherited neurological disorder which is characterised by involuntary tics. These tics are motor tics, the most common being eye squinting, facial grimacing or head shaking, and vocal and/or facial tics, the most common being throat clearing, lip smacking or sniffing. Although fairly rare, vocal tics may manifest themselves in socially unacceptable or inappropriate words or phrases, such as swearing. The usual age for these tics to appear is around 4 to 5 years and often it can be at its most severe at between the 10 and 12 years of age, but can improve into adolescence and adulthood. It does affect boys more frequently than girls and although medication can help the severity and frequency of the tics, as yet there is no permanent cure.

Associated difficulties may be ADD, AD/HD, Obsessive Compulsive Disorder (OCD) and various learning difficulties and depending on the severity of these will determine the educational provision of the pupil.

In our schools, to many of the other pupils, this affliction is quite humorous, but to those who actually have it, there is nothing funny about it. People with Tourette's Syndrome are on the whole unable to control their actions, and what is not needed is teasing and harassing. Again, as has been the whole theme of this book, understanding is such an important factor.

Top tips: Tourette's Syndrome

- Minimise stressful situations as stress can play a part in the frequency and severity of the tics

- Increase understanding and tolerance of other pupils, perhaps in circle time activities

- Provide a place to go if the pupil needs to exit the room quickly when the onset of a bout of tics occurs

- Ensure as far as possible, that the pupil has positive self esteem

Chapter Ten

Children who Challenge Us

'Their behaviour is telling us something; behaviour never says nothing.'
Rob Long & Jonathan Fogell

In your role as a teacher or teaching assistant there will be many times when you find your abilities, skills and personality will be tested. In no areas will this be more true than when you are working with pupils whose behaviour sometimes challenges us to the very limits.

But what exactly do we mean by that word, 'challenge'? What constitutes a challenge to one person may not be seen as a problem at all to another. Similarly, behaviour that is seen to be challenging in one setting or school may not be seen to be so challenging in another. Behaviour is considered to be challenging when it is perceived to be inappropriate in a particular situation.

So what, then, is inappropriate behaviour? All of us live by rules or standards. Schools create their own set of rules which helps uphold a particular ethos. What is deemed to be correct and important, therefore, in one school may not be a focus in another. Thus you cannot define the phrase 'inappropriate behaviour' divorced from the setting in which it is taking place. However, when a pupil presents a behaviour which affects the learning or safety of other people in any setting, this would always be termed inappropriate.

In addition to the setting there will be reasons why certain pupils behave as they do. Everybody behaves for a reason. Behaviour is a means for us to express what we are feeling or thinking. It is a form of communication.

Very often we only deal with the observable behaviour rather than stepping back and analysing the cause. Rigorous and frequent observations are important to establish these causes and also analyse the consequences.

Several methods have been developed over the years to help us with this, but most include the following points:

- *Where the behaviour happens or happened.* Ask yourself is there a pattern? Do the behaviours tend to happen in a certain place or at a certain time or with particular people?

- *What sparks it off?* Does anything observable happen to trigger that particular behaviour? For example, when a pupil is not chosen for a particular responsibility or quite simply, they are told they cannot do something they wish to.

- *What actually happens?* What is the behaviour like? What do they do? For example, they might be verbally aggressive or even physically aggressive, to adults, peers or property.

- *What do they get out of it?* This is a really important factor, as most of us behave for personal gain.

Recording of behaviours in this way must be very explicit if it is to be useful for developing positive interventions. For example, simply writing down that a pupil is aggressive is not enough. Recording that he pushed another pupil forcibly in the back whilst he took the ball will give a much clearer picture of the behaviour. Once you have gathered evidence such as this over a period of time, you will be able to analyse it and hopefully start to gain an insight into the problem and to concentrate on solutions.

Let's look back to our imaginary class. Some of those pupils were behaving in a way which made it difficult for the teacher. However, as we discussed, a knowledge of the underlying difficulties facing those pupils would have helped the teacher understand the reasons for those behaviours.

Once again it is so important that we take the time to consider the nature of the pupil's difficulties or any Special Educational Needs.

Remember, most pupils with SEN, particularly those with learning difficulties, will also have some degree of language and communication difficulty. Therefore the pupil who has problems understanding the language used around him in school and who may not be able to express himself efficiently may behave in an unexpected and unacceptable way without realising.

Pupils with ASD, through their poor social and communication skills can have their behaviour misinterpreted as defiant or rude. Others with ASD who get anxious or stressed but are maybe unable to express themselves adequately could display violence and aggression.

Classically, the pupil with AD/HD has usually acquired the label 'naughty'. However, if you consider that the three main characteristics of AD/HD are poor attention, impulsiveness and hyperactivity then it's little wonder that these pupils fall foul of school rules.

However, even though we know that there is a good reason for certain pupils' behaviours, such as those above, this is not an excuse for accepting the behaviours, nor for allowing them to continue. All inappropriate behaviours must be tackled, whatever the cause, but we need to be flexible in our approach. Let's look at a couple of case studies.

Danny, a six-year-old boy refuses to get changed for PE. His behaviour was interpreted as defiance by the school staff. In fact, this pupil, once he had taken his clothes off, was unable to put his other clothes on again in the correct order due to sequencing difficulties. This difficulty pervaded all areas of school life and impacted on his behaviour. Once it was established that sequencing skills were a major obstacle for him, strategies were put into place to help. In this instance, simple visual supports helped guide him through the process, which greatly reduced his anxiety and he was then happy enough to get changed for PE.

Stacey, a twelve-year-old girl, was consistently refusing to complete written work, was deemed to be lazy by subject teachers and was regularly given after school detentions. She began storming out of classes when there was the expectation of written work. Although teachers knew she had handwriting difficulties, they did not realise the extent of them and how much they hindered her efforts. The knock-on effects of her self esteem were getting worse as she was getting older. Her reputation as a difficult pupil was growing. A learning mentor spent time with Stacey, talking through her troubles and began to understand the extent of her writing difficulties and how much they were making her feel negative about most aspects of school. By allowing Stacey to use a word processor wherever possible, and building time into the week to teach her keyboarding skills, the pressure was taken off and her attitude improved.

Both of these cases highlight how by identifying the underlying causes of what seem to be, on the surface, difficult behaviours, an appropriate solution can be found which makes the difference.

Many pupils displaying poor behaviour will have social or emotional issues impacting on all areas of their lives; home, family, friends, and school. Poverty, neglect, family breakdown, and abuse all contribute to disturbed emotions and resulting behaviour problems. Children with these types of background problems are often the hardest to reach and understand by school staff as their difficulties may stem from circumstances which are beyond our control. However, even this does not exempt these pupils from following school rules and there should be high expectations from staff.

You might feel quite alone and inadequate when you first meet pupils who challenge. You might be tempted to take the confrontation or insult personally. However, it is vital that you recognise that these pupils rarely harbour personal grudges; it is far more likely that they are expressing a hurt or an anger that they feel against someone or something else, and you just happened to be in the wrong place at the wrong time! Even though the pupil's anger may have been directed at you it is important that this does not affect your future relationship with him. Therefore, once the behaviour has been dealt with, repair and rebuild that relationship positively. Start each day with a clean slate!

Don't forget that all schools are required to have a behaviour policy, which will outline the systems, structures, rewards and sanctions that have been established in the school. Tackling behaviour should be a team approach and staff should never feel they are working on their own. Below we have suggested some useful tips and strategies which may be helpful to remember if you find yourself in a difficult situation.

Top tips: Behaviour

- Wherever possible try and find out the cause of the behaviour and address the cause
- Be non-confrontational. Don't raise your voice.
- Emphasise and reinforce the behaviours you want, not the ones you don't want
- Aim to distract attention away from the behaviour
- Allow time to respond to your request
- Don't discuss the problem in the heat of the moment
- Forgive and forget. Don't take it personally.
- Tell the pupil you don't like the behaviour, not that you don't like him. Start your comments with 'I' ... .
- Follow through all sanctions – consistency is the key
- Deal with low level behaviours before they escalate
- Occasionally, some behaviours are better ignored, especially when the pupil is seeking attention
- Don't enter into debate or argument
- Be careful about tackling a pupil's behaviour in front of others; often it is best dealt with without an audience
- Watch your language – explain instructions and consequences clearly and simply
- Be firm. Be fair. Keep calm!

Chapter Eleven

The Jargon Jungle!

As this is an Educational journey, one might well expect, at some point, to travel through a dense area of jungle – jargon jungle! Most professions rely on the mystique of jargon to help their own internal communication systems. It provides a common vocabulary for those 'in the know', but of course, for those outside the profession, it may appear confusing or even intimidating.

Therefore, for those who are either new to, or unfamiliar with the jargon, we will spend a little time clearing the way and explaining some of the most frequently used terminology for you.

To begin with, it is important to recognise that even within the UK there is a wide range of differing terminology used in different countries to describe the same things, people and systems. Scotland, and England & Wales both have separate education systems and organise themselves differently.

However, even within England & Wales, there are many regional variations and individual LEAs have developed their own range of jargon to describe their own staff and systems.

This journey is 'A Whistle-Stop Tour of Special Educational Needs'. We have already looked at and described some of the difficulties and disabilities which affect a proportion of our pupils in mainstream schools. All these pupils will have Special Educational Needs. However, they come under an even bigger umbrella, which is widely termed A.E.N., that is, 'Additional Educational Needs'. This larger grouping includes the additional following categories of pupils:

- Looked After Children
- Travellers
- Refugees
- Pupils with English as an additional language
- Expectant pupil mothers
- Young Carers
- Gifted and Talented pupils
- Bullied children

While these pupils may not have Special Educational Needs, they are considered to require additional support and help within school.

In Scotland, as we discussed on page 8, the move is very much towards the broader umbrella of social inclusion and considering a much wider range of needs such as those listed above. The new term 'Additional Support Needs' (ASN) is now used to refer to this broader range which may or may not include pupils with what have been known as special educational needs. The important thing to emphasise is that in Scotland ASN is not just a substitution for SEN but incorporates a much wider range, and the emphasis is on supporting needs rather than diagnosing problems.

So, Who's Who in Education and What do they do?

Countrywide, there are external professionals who work collaboratively with schools to give advice, support and help to both staff and pupils. Here is a list of some of the professionals you might see and need to liaise with:

Educational Psychologist – these are highly qualified professionals who are able to provide in-depth assessments of pupils and identify both strengths and weaknesses. They are permitted to use specific assessments not available for use by teachers. These often indicate a pupil's innate ability, rather than their achievement, which may have huge implications for the teaching methods in use in the class or school. Educational Psychologists offer invaluable advice to teachers on teaching styles and strategies for both individual pupils or whole class use. In addition, their role may be to deliver Special Educational Needs training to school staff, and even to parents.

Speech and Language Therapist – again, these are highly qualified professionals who may be employed either by education or, more usually, health. Schools may refer a pupil to a Speech and Language Therapist where they have concerns about the pupil's speech, or where they suspect the pupil has an underlying receptive or expressive language difficulty or delay. These therapists will use specialised assessments to pinpoint the specific difficulty and then suggest appropriate intervention programmes and strategies. In many schools nowadays, the delivery of these programmes falls to school staff. Usually, there will be training offered to schools by the therapists to assist this process.

Physiotherapist – highly trained and usually employed by health, their role is to identify and help remedy gross motor movement difficulties by the provision of a therapeutic programme. Those therapists choosing to work with children will often know the child's case from an early age and will have received the referral through the health system. However, when a child reaches school age, the physiotherapist may liaise with school staff and hand over the delivery of the programme to them. Physiotherapy programmes usually need to be carried out 'little and often'. The physiotherapist herself will monitor the programme and progress of the pupil.

Occupational Therapist (OT) – another highly trained professional employed by health who specialises in difficulties with fine motor movements, i.e. upper body movements, posture and manual dexterity. Nowadays teachers are alert to the possibility of pupils having Dyspraxia and may feel the need to refer to an OT, either directly or via the pupil's family General Practitioner. OTs will be able to assess and advise on the range of fine motor difficulties and like the other therapists will provide and monitor a therapeutic programme which is usually carried out in school. They will often advise on the use of educational aids and equipment, e.g. chairs, adapted desks or specialist writing tools.

Advisory Teachers – all LEAs will have different titles for these professionals, but whatever they are called, they are teachers who have experience and expertise in a specified area of SEN. This might be in ASD (Autism Spectrum Disorder), Cognition and Learning (by cognition we mean the mental processes which enable us to learn), Physical and Sensory difficulties, SEBD (Social, Emotional and Behavioural Difficulties) and Specific Learning difficulties. Usually they are employed by the LEAs and have a caseload of schools. They will be able to assess pupils, advise, support and train school staff. In each LEA the structure and system of working for these professionals will vary.

The SEN Code of Practice (England & Wales) (CoP)

This is the school's 'bible' for all matters relating to SEN. The latest edition was published in November 2001 and is the government's guide to a school's statutory obligations to pupils with SEN and their parents. It covers the processes and framework that needs to be in place if schools are to identify, assess, support and monitor their SEN pupils successfully. The SENCo and head teacher will have most cause to refer to this document and all schools in England and Wales will have at least one copy. Although it may not be necessary for class teachers and Teaching Assistants to know the CoP in depth it is advisable to both know where it is and have at least a broad oversight of it.

Let's tease out some of the pertinent points of the Code of Practice and to illustrate the 'Staged Approach' we will take one of our imaginary pupils, Lucy, through the procedure.

Right back in Reception Class Lucy's teacher was aware that her development in several areas, i.e. language, fine motor and cognition (as evidenced by the lack of progress with basic literacy and numeracy skills) was significantly delayed in comparison with the other pupils in the class. After discussions about Lucy's lack of progress with the SENCo, it was agreed that there should be a meeting with Lucy's parents and that she would be placed on the SEN register at the:

- SCHOOL ACTION stage – This means that school is aware of her difficulties but feels that with well differentiated work and close monitoring of her progress her needs may be met within class.

They agree to review the situation after two terms by which time Lucy will be in year 1. The pace of the curriculum has increased slightly and the gap is widening between Lucy's level of achievement and her peers. Her class teacher suspects that she is having difficulty understanding much of the language being used in class and cannot easily follow instructions. A referral is made by the SENCo to the Speech and Language Therapy Service. They identify a Receptive language delay and provide a therapeutic programme.

Lucy's parents are both supportive and concerned and have had frequent discussions both formally and informally with the teacher and the SENCo. It was further agreed that an additional referral should be made to the Advisory Teacher for Cognition and Learning for a detailed assessment and advice. The Advisory Teacher confirmed that Lucy had significant learning difficulties and suggested an intense intervention programme to target basic literacy and numeracy, which required a high level of adult input. At this point the school moved Lucy to:

- SCHOOL ACTION PLUS stage – It is usual for pupils at this stage to have had intervention and support from external professionals, to have an Individual Education Plan (IEP) and to be receiving a higher level of adult support. An IEP consists of a set of targets, usually three or four and up to a maximum of five. As the IEP should be reviewed approximately two or three times a year, targets should be succinct, clear and achievable within that timescale. These are often referred to as SMART targets: Small Measurable Achievable Realistic Time based.

  It is also likely that at this stage a pupil will need a greatly differentiated curriculum as the achievement gap between him and his peers will have widened. The IEP should only target areas of need which are very different from or outside the differentiated class curriculum. Continued active intervention will be needed if the gap is not to widen further. You may also come across GEPs (group education plans), created for pupils with similar educational needs.

Lucy is coming to the end of Year 2 and has undergone a teacher assessment for her Key Stage 1 SATs. These have highlighted that although she has made some progress, she continues to experience significant difficulties in both literacy and numeracy and it is the judgement of all professionals and the wish of her parents that Lucy undergoes a statutory assessment to further ascertain the extent of her needs and the level of support she will be likely to need in the future. Therefore, the school initiated the process and having agreed, the LEA began to gather the evidence they would require to make an informed judgement. Lucy was then seen by an Educational Psychologist and had a medical and other advice was sought.

At the end of the process, the LEA, in this case, agreed that Lucy did require a:

- STATEMENT OF EDUCATIONAL NEED – The purpose of the collected evidence is to provide the LEA with as detailed a picture of the pupil as possible. Other services or therapists who have known or have worked with the pupil may also be asked to submit a report. The final decision to either issue a Statement or not, usually rests with a panel of senior professionals. The Code of Practice dictates time scales for the process from the receipt of the initial request through to the final decision and issue of the Statement itself. The Statement is a legal document which gives a detailed profile of the pupil's needs and educational requirements. It can also quantify and qualify support from specialist services and name appropriate placements.

With the recommended support in place from the Statement and ongoing external involvement, Lucy's progress is slow but steady in her mainstream setting. She continues to need a differentiated curriculum and with adult support she works hard on the targets from her IEP. Within a year, her parents, teacher, SENCo, head teacher and other involved professionals gather together at the:

- ANNUAL REVIEW – The purpose of this meeting, which takes place at least once a year, is to review the pupil's progress, set new annual targets for them and discuss whether the content of the Statement remains relevant to the needs of the pupil or if it requires amending. If necessary, the Statement can be reviewed more frequently, this may be because the pupil's level of need has altered significantly or perhaps a change in the support or provision is required.

It must be remembered that different Education Authorities have their own criteria in the various areas of SEN for issuing a statement.

If parents are not happy with the decision made by the local education authorities [LEAs] in England and Wales, they can appeal to the Special Educational Needs and Disability Tribunal [SENDIST]. The Tribunal is independent of both central and local government.

In Scotland, at present, the process of identification of needs follows a similar pattern to that described in the Code of Practice above. It is a collaborative process involving the class teacher, support for learning staff, parents and pupil. It may be possible to put in place a set of arrangements including additional support within school, and perhaps targets set in an Individualised Educational Programme (IEP) in order to support the teaching and learning. For some children with more complex long-term needs further intervention may be required. This is done through referral to an educational psychologist and it may be necessary to open a Record of Needs (similar to the Statement of Needs outlined above). The Record of Needs is a legal document which gives a detailed profile of the pupil's needs and educational requirements. It can also quantify and qualify support from specialist services and name placements.

It is important to note, however, that when the new Education (Additional Support for Learning) (Scotland) Act 2004 comes into force in autumn 2005 these arrangements will change as the Record of Needs will no longer be a part of the process. The new framework of support includes a Co-ordinated Support Plan (CSP) for pupils who have long term complex or multiple barriers to learning who require a range of support from different services outside education, e.g. health or social services. The CSP is a statutory document providing a long-term strategic plan for the child's learning. Anyone involved in supporting the learning needs will be able to be involved in drawing it up, reviewing it and implementing it. The education authority will have responsibility for the CSP but if appropriate, they may delegate this to an individual outside education, e.g. a health or social worker, if they have more close involvement with the child and the family.

It is important to recognise that the CSP is not a direct replacement for the Record of Needs, but will apply only to pupils who require input from a variety of agencies outside education to ensure that all their learning needs are addressed.

A new Code of Practice for Scotland will be published in 2005 to provide education authorities with guidelines for implementing the Act.

We hope that we have been able to clear a small pathway through the 'Jargon Jungle' for you but we would always recommend that you refer back to the Code of Practice for detailed advice.

However, we are going to sidetrack for a moment to ensure that we are all familiar with a term which we have used several times previously but which deserves a little more attention:

'PERSONALISED LEARNING' OR 'DIFFERENTIATION'

The term 'Personalised Learning' in the educational world has come to mean differentiating or adapting the standard curriculum to suit the needs of other smaller groups or even individual pupils. This can mean anything from extending and challenging pupils who are gifted and talented, to translating work into Braille for a pupil who is blind or selecting appropriate work tasks, resources and methods of delivery for a pupil with learning difficulties who is not able to achieve the level expected for their particular year group.

The importance of good differentiation and personalised work cannot be underestimated. It not only offers the increased possibility for the pupil to experience success, whatever their level, but that success in itself will have a positive effect on the pupil's own self esteem, motivation and very often, behaviour.

Just stop and take a moment to think how it would feel if you joined an evening class to study Advanced Nuclear Physics. With apologies to those of you reading this book who are Advanced Nuclear Physicists, the rest of us would soon be feeling confused, inadequate, fed up and excluded. Why? Because, firstly, you can't understand much of the language used in the lessons. You can pick up some, but miss too much of the essential technical vocabulary for it all to make sense. The lecturer seems to be speaking very quickly and each lesson is a different topic. You dread being given a written assignment as this will only show up how much you don't know! Looking around the class after a few weeks, you realise that most of the class is keeping up with the pace and this leaves you feeling left out and wanting to give up. Maybe you do.

Is this anybody's fault?

The lecturer is highly regarded in his field and is an excellent communicator.

The students are working well and seem to enjoy what they do.

Some of them are only too happy to offer you help with your assignments.

Are you at fault then? No, because you turned up regularly and tried your hardest. You really wanted to succeed.

The problem was that you didn't have enough previous knowledge, the work was therefore too hard and the pace was too quick.

Transfer this to the classroom of today, and it is easy to see how some pupils become disaffected. All of our imaginary pupils portrayed at the beginning of this book would benefit from careful and imaginative differentiation by their class teacher. We acknowledge that without a doubt, creating a personalised programme is a demanding and time-consuming process. There is no short cut although a wise teacher can build up and collect a bank of resources that they can then use again in the future.

Therefore, at the risk of repeating ourselves we need to reiterate the importance of an appropriate and creative adaptation to the curriculum for pupils whose progress in school depends on it.

So what yardstick are we to measure this progress by?

Chapter Twelve

National Curriculum

In schools in England and Wales we work under the guidelines set out in the National Curriculum. All pupils follow the National Curriculum and only a very small number are disapplied.

This was first introduced in 1988. It brought a structure to the teaching of all subjects from Reception year to the end of Key Stage 3. Teachers had to work within a framework and timescale in each area. Progress through the Curriculum was marked by attainment levels. These ranged from Levels 1 to 8. Until recently, pupils who could not attain Level 1 were said to be 'Working Towards Level 1' (known as 'W'). Many pupils, therefore, spent a large part of their school career never moving off 'W', which meant that any progress they had made was not measurable through the National Curriculum assessment framework. This was discouraging for all involved; teachers, parents and the pupils themselves.

Chapter Thirteen

P Scales

Within the last five years the Government introduced the Performance Scales, now commonly known as the 'P Scales'. These are statements of performance linked to childhood development, and progress from the earliest infantile responses, P1, through to P8 in each subject, from which a pupil moves smoothly onto Level 1c of the National Curriculum. In other words, the P Scales have replaced the 'W' level by breaking it down into very small steps and progress can be shown as the pupil moves up through each P Scale.

This has had a welcome and positive impact for those of us working with pupils with SEN, as we now have a standardised means of assessment to show that even the least able pupils are making progress. There is an ever-increasing range of commercial materials and resources to help teachers plan for the next stage and set realistic targets.

Chapter Fourteen

The Scottish Curriculum Framework

The Scottish curriculum framework has been designed as a framework for all, including pupils with special educational needs. It consists of a series of curriculum guidelines and suggested programmes of study for 3 – 5, 5 – 14 (including the Elaborated 5 – 14 curriculum), Standard Grade and the National Qualifications.

The Elaborated 5 – 14 curriculum framework and associated programmes of study was specifically designed to meet the needs of pupils who have severe, profound and complex learning difficulties. These are learners who may be 'working towards' Level A of the main 5 – 14 framework for their whole school career. The Elaborated 5 – 14 framework offers a series of seven steps in each of six key curriculum elements which dovetail into the key curriculum areas within the main 5 –14 framework.

The Elaborated curriculum enables teachers to plan an appropriately challenging curriculum for these learners and the framework provides a means of assessing and reporting meaningfully on achievement and progression.

The National Qualifications were introduced in the mid-nineties as an inclusive curriculum framework for pupils aged sixteen plus. It incorporates Higher Still Access modules at levels 1, 2 and 3 which are accessible for pupils with special educational needs. Access level 1 is particularly designed with the needs of learners with severe and complex needs in mind ensuring that all learners are enabled to have their curriculum achievements recognised through national certification.

The Raising Standards – Setting Targets initiative 1999 was also intended to include pupils with special educational needs and the Success for All Handbook (2000) provided detailed advice on setting appropriately challenging targets in IEPs that are located within the national curriculum framework.

More recently, Circular No. 3/2001 (Guidance on Flexibility in the Curriculum) gives further advice to enable schools to address the wide range of learning needs and contexts to *'ensure that all young people have the opportunity to achieve their full potential'*.

Chapter Fifteen

Being Professional

The last and final stage of our journey on this Whistle-Stop Tour is intended to remind ourselves of the importance of our role as professionals who have an impact on the lives of the children and young people we work within our schools today.

Anyone who works in a school is part of a team. This certainly has its advantages, as in most circumstances there are other people around who can share your 'highs and lows'. The creative possibilities are far more than the sum of its individual members. Being a team member, however, means we have shared responsibilities and are mutually accountable. By their very nature, SEN pupils often require extra support and help from numerous staff, both internal and external, and usually generate a lot of paperwork. Good communication, close liaison and collaborative working are essential to provide a high quality bespoke educational programme for pupils.

The Government's Code of Practice quite clearly states that:

'All teachers are teachers of children with special educational needs.'
(5:2 Code of Practice 2001)

It is no longer a question of class teachers referring their SEN pupils on to the SENCo, SfL or SEN teacher and seeing their education as someone else's responsibility. The implications of this on class management are huge and require finely honed collaboration between the class teacher, teaching assistants and other professionals who are involved with the pupil.

Although each member of staff will have clearly identified roles within the school, mutual respect for each others' skills and expertise is essential.

In most classrooms nowadays the teacher will be assisted by at least one teaching assistant. The class teacher is ultimately responsible for what goes on in the class, in terms of delivery of the curriculum, ensuring and monitoring progress for all pupils, and behaviour management. As we have already noted, the teacher is responsible for ensuring that pupils with SEN have their needs met and are included in all aspects of class life. In reality this means identifying and understanding the pupil's needs and striving to provide learning experiences that will enable the pupil to progress. This might be through adaptations to the working environment, differentiated or personalised learning in different subjects as necessary, or the use of alternative methods of presentation in order to maximise a pupil's preferred learning style.

Learning styles are most normally categorised as visual, auditory and kinaesthetic (doing). Although, a more appropriate sequence for many SEN children would be kinaesthetic, auditory/visual. Some teachers like to divide them up further into eight different types of learner: linguistic (good with words), bodily/kinaesthetic, logical/mathematical, naturalistic (like to interact learning with surroundings), spatial, interpersonal (like learning with others), musical, and intrapersonal (like to work alone).

The teaching assistant's role will vary from school to school. As a general comment, however, it is true to say that in most situations the teaching assistant will be there to help facilitate the teaching and learning in general and in many cases with SEN pupils in particular.

The following tips might be useful for consideration in order to create a positive team spirit:

Top tips: School

- Make sure everyone is clear about their role within the school and within the class
- The teacher needs to make sure other staff have essential information about SEN pupils
- Establish a time in the week to liaise with everyone
- Share knowledge and expertise gained from any professional development, training etc.
- Share objectives and content of lesson ideally before it begins
- Be very clear about who does what paperwork
- Establish ground rules for marking and annotating work
- Always ensure a pupil's work is dated
- Share with each other all relevant information that could affect the pupil's learning and behaviour
- Have shared expectations for the pupil
- Support each other in any behavioural issues
- Maintain a professional attitude with each other at all times in front of the pupils
- A good sense of humour works wonders!

Keeping yourself Safe

Working with children and young people today requires one to have integrity and common sense. It cannot be emphasised enough that staff must not allow themselves to be drawn into any situation which may be misconstrued by others. This is particularly important to remember when dealing with pupils who may be emotionally vulnerable. Sometimes modern day influences can encourage young people to rebel against those who work with them. Since the abolition of corporal punishment in schools, we have moved into a situation where it is expected that school staff will not handle pupils physically except in extenuating circumstances. This will be where a pupil is in danger of harming himself or others. There will also be times when a pupil may have to be restrained for the above reasons, but all schools will have a policy regarding this and where behaviour may be an issue for a school, staff are likely to receive training for positive handling.

If you find yourself in a situation where you have to talk to a pupil regarding their behaviour, or some other sensitive issue, it would always be advisable to ensure that whenever possible you are not doing this alone. Wherever you are, try and have a colleague within earshot.

Child Protection is one of the most sensitive issues within a school and requires the highest level of confidentiality. All schools will have a designated Child Protection Officer and you need to know who that person is. There will also be a Child Protection Policy in place. Briefly, abuse can be divided into four categories, physical abuse, sexual abuse, emotional abuse and neglect. All are equally serious and can have devastating long-term effects on people's lives. It is our responsibility to be vigilant and observant but not jump to any conclusions.

If you ever find yourself in the situation where a pupil discloses disturbing information, the following points are important to remember:

- Let the pupil know that he's done the right thing by telling you
- Listen carefully to the pupil; do not probe for further information

- Do *not* make a promise to the pupil that you won't tell anyone else; explain to them that you may have to talk to other people who will be able to help

- Again reassure the pupil and explain what you are going to do next

- Write down everything the pupil has disclosed as soon as you can, using the pupil's own words if possible, and being as accurate as possible. Do not put your own interpretation upon it. Sign it and record the date and exact time of the conversation

- Pass on this information to the designated Child Protection Officer immediately

- Under *no* circumstances must you relay the content of the conversation and information to anyone else, including colleagues.

Similarly, if you suspect or have only vague concerns that a pupil is experiencing any kind of abuse, make a note of it and pass on these concerns to the Child Protection Officer. Child Protection records are highly confidential and under the supervision of the Child Protection Officer.

Chapter Sixteen

The End of The Tour

We've come a long way since the start of the book and have tried to cover a large number of topics in the world of SEN. Once again, as the title clearly states, this book is not an exhaustive study of special educational needs.

Rather we have offered a broad oversight of the issues most pertinent to a teacher or teaching assistant who is new to or unfamiliar with special educational needs. This book is only a starting point; we sincerely hope that reading this will have whet your appetite to look further into areas of particular interest to you.

We have included useful reminders in the form of the 'Top Tips' so they can be easily referred back to. The website addresses will prove useful for further research and enquiry.

This book is the product of the experience of many years work with pupils who have SEN, in different settings, together with continuing professional interest and a desire to share what we have learnt with others.

We hope you feel this Whistle-Stop Tour has been worthwhile!

Chapter Seventeen

Useful Websites

Here are some websites which offer very useful information for both professionals and families on issues relating to Special Educational Needs.

ADDiss Information Services	www.addiss.co.uk
Afasic (Language Impaired Children)	www.afasic.org.uk
Association for Spina Bifida and Hydrocephalus	www.asbah.org
Behaviour	www.roblong.co.uk
Capability Scotland	www.capability-scotland.org.uk
Children in Scotland	www.childreninscotland.org.uk
Contact a Family	www.cafamily.org.uk
Contact a Family Scotland	www.cafamily.org.uk/scotland
Contact a Family Wales	www.cafamily.org.uk/wales
Contact a Family Northern Ireland	www.cafamily.org.uk/nireland
Department for Education and Skills	www.dfes.gov.uk
Disability Equipment	http://www.benefitsnowshop.co.uk
Dyscalculia	www.dyscalculia.org
The Dyslexia Institute	www.dyslexia-inst.org.uk
Dyslexia in Scotland	www.dyslexia-in-scotland.org
The British Dyslexia Association	www.bda-dyslexia.org.uk
The Dyspraxia Foundation	www.dyspraxiafoundation.org.uk

Down's Syndrome Association	www.downs-syndrome.org.uk
Down's Syndrome Scotland	www.dsscotland.org.uk
Enquire	www.enquire.org.uk
I Can	www.ican.org.uk
	www.talkingpoint.org.uk
Irlen Syndrome	www.irlen.co.uk
Learning and Teaching Scotland	www.LTScotland.org.uk/inclusiveeducation
Mencap (Learning Disability)	www.mencap.org.uk
National Autistic Society	www.nas.org.uk
QCA	www.qca.org.uk
Royal National Institute for the Blind	www.rnib.org.uk
Royal National Institute for the Deaf	www.rnid.org.uk
Scope (Cerebral Palsy)	www.scope.org.uk
Scottish Centre for Children with Motor Impairments	www.craighalbert.co.uk
Scottish Executive website	www.scotland.gov.uk
Scottish Society for Autism	www.autism-in-scotland.org.uk
Special Educational Needs & Disability Tribunal	http://www.sendist.gov.uk
Teachernet	www.teachernet.gov.uk
Tourette Syndrome (UK) Association	www.tsa.org.uk
Tourette Scotland	www.cwgsy.net/community/tosy/scotland/index.htm

Index